At the Shops

Leon Read

W

FRANKLIN WATTS
LONDON•SYDNEY

Contents

Shopping list   4

Getting money   6

Let's go shopping   8

Finding things   10

At the checkout   12

Buying food   14

Heavy bags   16

Buying on-line   18

Let's play shop   20

My High Street   22

Word picture bank   24

Look out for Tiger on the pages of this book. Sometimes he is hiding.

Today, Adele is going to the shops
with her mum and little sister.

Shopping list

Adele has helped her mum to make a shopping list.

make - up
toothbrush
bananas
watermelon
peaches
ham
cheese
CD

Mum puts her bag in the car.
The girls get into the car.

Getting money

In town, Mum gets some of her money from a cashpoint.

Adele takes
out the money.

Then she puts
the money into
Mum's purse.

Why does Mum
keep the money
in her purse?

Let's go shopping

There are lots of shops
in the High Street.

First, Mum takes Adele and her sister to the chemist.

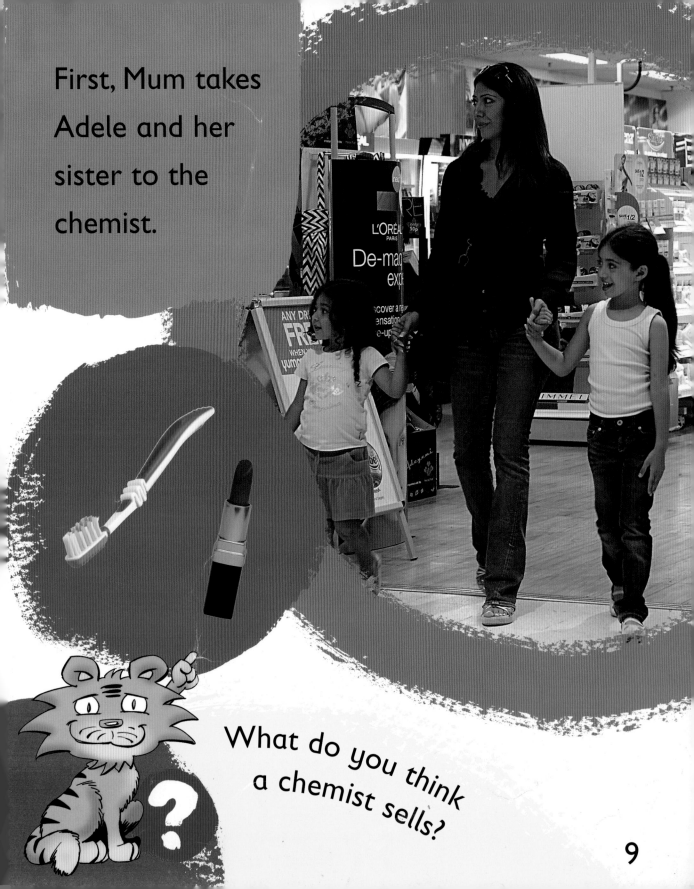

What do you think a chemist sells?

9

Finding things

Adele finds Mum's make-up on a shelf.

Then they look for a toothbrush.

Adele's sister has found something she wants.

No, you can't buy it. Please put it back.

What things have you bought at a chemist?

At the checkout

Adele pays at the checkout.

She gives the assistant £20.

£20

The make-up and toothbrush cost £8.99.

The assistant gives Adele back £11.01 in change.

Buying food

At the food store, Mum checks the shopping list. They need bananas.

Adele gets the peaches, then Mum finds the watermelon.

They try some cheese before they buy it. Then Mum buys the ham.

Why should you make a shopping list?

Heavy bags

The girls help to carry the
shopping bags to the car.

It has been a long day.
Mum decides to buy
the CD on-line.

Can you remember what items they have bought?

Buying on-line

At home, Adele helps Mum to buy
a CD from an on-line shop.

A couple of days later the CD
is delivered to Adele's home.

Thank you.

What have you helped
your mum or dad
to buy on-line?

19

Let's play shop

Adele has written a pretend shopping list.

She goes to her sister's shop.

Adele looks at her list. She finds the things she needs.

Here is your change.

She pays for everything at the checkout.

My High Street

Adele and her sister are using boxes to make their own High Street.

They have made:

a toy shop,

a cake shop,

a music shop,

and a fruit shop.

What shops would you put in your High Street?

Word picture bank

Cashpoint – P. 6

Change – P. 13, 21

Checkout – P. 12, 21

Chemist – P. 9, 10

High Street – P. 8, 22, 23

On-line – P. 17, 18

First published in 2008 by Franklin Watts
338 Euston Road, London NW1 3BH

Franklin Watts Australia
Level 17/207 Kent Street, Sydney NSW 2000

Copyright © Franklin Watts 2008

Series editor: Adrian Cole
Photographer: Andy Crawford (unless otherwise credited)
Design: Sphere Design Associates
Art director: Jonathan Hair
Consultants: Prue Goodwin and Karina Law

A CIP catalogue record for this book is available
from the British Library.

ISBN: 978 0 7496 7620 9

Dewey Classification: 381'.1

Acknowledgements:
The Publisher would like to thank Norrie Carr model agency,
Superdrug PLC, Woolworths, and Pirno, Carmelo and Assunta
at Italian Continental Stores Limited.
'Tiger' puppet used with kind permission from Ravensden PLC
(www.ravensden.co.uk).
Tiger Talk logo drawn by Kevin Hopgood.

Shutterstock (4, 9c and cl).

Every attempt has been made to clear copyright.
Should there be any inadvertent omission please
apply to the publisher for rectification.

Printed in China

Franklin Watts is a division
of Hachette Children's Books,
an Hachette Livre UK company.

There are 19 Tigers, including me, in this book. Did you find all of us?